Stoats in the Sunlight

Poems by Stewart Conn

STOATS
IN THE
SUNLIGHT

 HUTCHINSON OF LONDON

Hutchinson & Co. (Publishers) Ltd
178–202 Great Portland Street, London W1

London Melbourne Sydney
Auckland Bombay Toronto
Johannesburg New York

First published 1968
© *Stewart Conn 1968*

09 087710 1

This book has been set in Bembo, printed in Great Britain
on Antique Wove paper by Benham and Company Limited, Colchester, Essex,
and bound by Wm. Brendon and Son Limited, of Tiptree, Essex

To my Parents

1

2

Acknowledgment is made to *Akros, The Glasgow Herald, Liberté* (Canada), *Lines, The Listener, New Saltire, The Observer, Outposts, Poet, Poetry Review, Quicksilver, The Scotsman, Scottish Field, Transatlantic Review,* and to the B.B.C., for poems broadcast on the Home Service and Third Programme. Also to *Modern Scottish Poetry* (Faber), *P.E.N. New Poems '65* (Hutchinson), *Scottish Poetry 1 & 2* (Edinburgh University Press), *The Scottish Literary Revival* (Collier–Macmillan), *Young Commonwealth Poets '65* (Heinemann), *New Voices of the Commonwealth* (Evans Brothers). I should like to express my gratitude to the E. C. Gregory (Leeds) Trustees.

1

TODD

My father's white uncle became
   Arthritic and testamental in
   Lyrical stages. He held cardinal sin
Was misuse of horses, then any game

Won on the sabbath. A Clydesdale
   To him was not bells and sugar or declension
   From paddock, but primal extension
Of rock and soil. Thundered nail

Turned to sacred bolt. And each night
   In the stable he would slaver and slave
   At cracked hooves, or else save
Bowls of porridge for just the right

Beast. I remember I lied
   To him once, about oats: then I felt
   The brand of his loving tongue, the belt
Of his own horsey breath. But he died,

When the mechanised tractor came to pass.
   Now I think of him neighing to some saint
   In a simple heaven or, beyond complaint,
Leaning across a fence and munching grass.

THE ORCHARD

Loose-rigged, the orchard pitches
Like a sailing-ship caught on the swell
Of slapdash southern seas. Cargoes burst
In the hold, under canvas or barrel

On barrel piled high. And the sun
Is the colour of straw; and the sky,
Yanked brutally in, leaves heaps
Of apples rotting where they lie.

A drugged light swills the poop. Trees,
Mast and yard-arm, take the strain.
Air's bruised. Rain litters the yellow
Deck, then swabs it clear again.

Crushed branch, made flashing bowsprit,
Slithers under. Mashed shapes shoot
Through spindrift. Crude as Caliban,
Pigs stuff their filthy bellies and root

For more. Yet I remember
A simpler order in this place:
When boys in azure tunics climbed
Flimsy ladders and stepped out into space.

'HARELAW'

Ploughlands roll where limekilns lay
  Seeping in craters. Where once dense
  Fibres oozed against gatepost and fence
Till staples burst, firm wheatfields sway;
  And where quarries reeked, intense

With honeysuckle, a truck dumps load
  Upon load of earth, of ash and slag
  For the raking. Spliced hawsers drag
Roots out and wrench the rabbit wood
  Apart as though some cuckoo fugue

Had rioted. On this mossy slope
  That raindrops used to drill and drum
  Through dusk, no nightjar flits nor numb
Hawk hangs as listening foxes lope
  And prowl; no lilac shadows thumb

The heavy air. This holt was mine
  To siege and plunder; here I caged
  Rare beasts or swayed royally on the agèd
Backs of horses—here hacked my secret sign,
  Strode, wallowed, ferreted, rampaged.

But acres crumple and the farm's new image
  Spreads over the old. As I face
  Its change, a truck tips litter; hens assess
Bright tins, then peck and squawk their rage.
  The truck spurts flame and I have no redress.

STRANGE SERAPH

(*for Neil M. Gunn*)

A cart-horse clumps up Broughton Street,
Pounding the dun cobbles into themselves
With hooves like hammers that beat
Sparks where the causeway shelves
To the gutter. Carved head slung back,
Clamped mouth showing teeth, he reeks
Of effort: smooth shoulders, black
And varnished, ply a rhythm that speaks

Its proven purpose. On his wide
Forehead, a star—with bright
Harness making horse strange seraph tied
To 'here' and 'now' by shafts of light.
A shoe skliffs. Partly thrown
Off balance, he is jerked upright
By crupper and chain. Foam blown
Finely from nostrils wreathes his sight,

As he grapples to contemplate
White fields' more true environment
With no thwacking coalman to berate
Him, but what he himself would invent.
For this Edinburgh is to him
Neither garden city nor Elysium.
With nothing for it but to drag the dream
Along, he stamps and lets off clouds of steam.

TIME WITHIN TIME

A lobster-boat slops in the Minch,
  Surrounded by creels. Ropes,
Wriggling rainbows, inch
  Their cargo up. The red deck slopes;

Oars drip; the sail's quick
  Parchment. With an ease
More Greek than Gaelic,
  She trails through stainless seas

Towards the hills of Harris. There
  Cold economics will be blind
To metaphor and myth: yet where
  Can these be safely left behind?

So, as they go, old Iain sees
  Himself with eagles on his fist;
While Neil at the mast's Ulysses,
  Cramping his mighty bow against his wrist.

AYRSHIRE FARM

Every new year's morning the farmers
Would meet at 'Harelaw' with their guns
For the shoot. Mungo red in the face,
Matthew hale as a tree, John huge
In old leather. The others in dribs
And drabs, shotguns over their shoulders,
Bags flopping at their sides, collars up.

We'd set out across the north park,
The glaur on our leggings freezing
As we left the shelter of the knowes.
No dogs. Even the ferrets on this day
Of days were left squealing behind
Their wire. We'd fan out, taking
The slope at a steady tramp.

Mungo always aimed first, blasting away
At nothing. Hugh cursed under his breath;
The rest of us kept going. Suddenly
The hares would rise from the bracken-clumps
And go looping downhill. I remember
The banks alive with scuts, the dead
Gorse-tufts splattered with shot.

One by one the haversacks filled,
The blood dripping from them, staining
The snow. Matthew still in front,
Directing the others; the sun red
Behind its dyke, the wind rising.
And myself bringing up the rear,
Pretending I was lost, become the quarry.

Three blasts on a whistle, the second
Time round. And, in from the sleet,
We would settle on bales with bottles
And flasks, to divide the spoils. The bodies
Slit, and hung on hooks to drip. The rest
Thrown smoking on the midden. The dogs
Scrabbling on their chains, Todd's stallion

Rearing at the reek of blood. Then in
To the fire and a roaring new year:
Old Martha and Mima scuffling to and fro,
Our men's bellies filling, hands
Slowly thawing. And for me, off to bed,
A pig in the sheets, the oil lamp
Throwing shadows of rabbits on the wall.

★

Last winter I covered the same ground
On my own, no gun. Old Martha and Mima
Have gone to rest. Todd has tethered
His horses under the hill. Mungo, too,
From a fall at the baling. Yet my breathing
Seemed to make their shapes; and Matthew's
And Hugh's, and my own bringing up the rear.

At the road-end I stopped and stood
For some time, just listening. My hands
Growing numb. Then I crossed the track
To where a single rabbit lay twitching,
Big-headed, eyes bulging, in pain.
I took the heaviest stone I could find;
And with one blow beat in its brains.

AFTERNOON

I lying on lichen can see
rivulets glancing in the sun
like fishes' scales or silver
sixpences. I rise and run

downhill until I reach a pool
wedged innocently between
two rocks, where lazy lizards slide
as if afraid of being seen

by heron or tell-tale poet. Then
a tasselled waterfall
that holds its breath only to spill
spindrift my thoughts. Suddenly all

grows quiet, as if today
as fossil has been overlapped
by some tomorrow only five
senses away but not yet mapped.

RAT CATCHER

Farm-lands his larder he settles with
   Stallions or, bedded in hay, brings
Colour to loft and stall. Sleek shapes
   Come grinning at the songs he sings.

He lets them swarm, then wets his knife
   Along their throats. Shiny with sweat
He fastens on. Immortal catcher,
   He snaps their bones under his feet.

Then lanterns are lit, and the steading
   Roars like a forge. But he'll creep
Between layers of sack, take
   A swig, and hump himself to sleep.

With no ear for music, his own tune
   Has him baffled. Nor does he understand
When they catch their children drinking
   From the well of his cupped hand.

So he swaggers into the sun, is black
   Upon red, slap-happy harlequin;
Or, splashing through legendary fields,
   Heads for some other unknown Hamelin.

THE CLEARING

Woodsmoke, sheer grape-bloom, smears
The trunks of trees, tricks larches
Lilac, and as deftly clears.
Startingly, among patches
Of sunlight, come glints
Of steel: the woodmen are at
It early. Red-jerkined, gigantic
In quirk lighting, they flit

Under branches, make markings
Or, smirched, become blurs
Of themselves. Somewhere a dog barks.
Hand-saws spark, and sputter.
Breaking cover, a brood
Of partridges wheedles
Through charlock. Lopped wood,
Crippling down, sends needles

Showering. Blades whurr; logs are
Rolled and chained. Crushed
Brushwood leaks. Air
Is spiced with resin and sawdust.
Then they are gone, to the sound
Of singing. Where pathways join,
Fires flicker. And the ground
Is littered with huge and copper coins.

CRAIGIE HILL

I once came across a pack of stoats in the sunlight,
Their eyes like jewels, the tips of their tails black.

One kept swinging on a fencepost and springing
To the ground, leaving the wires twanging.

As at a word of command, they took up
Close formation and moved off in one direction.

Knowing what I do now, I wouldn't have stood there
Watching, imagining them such dainty playthings.

TWO STUDIES

1   For a Highland Preacher

Others of his calling wheeze
   Through extension of metaphor
   And preach a sheepish fire,
Then are put out to graze
Within the bounds of a rope's
   Wheeling or, frayed in mind
   And body, are finally drowned
In their own saintly shapes.

Not this for him. Dynamic,
   He glares all sermons with
   The clear unblustering faith
That defines his gaelic
Bearing. Under shiny robes
   His thumping blacksmith's arm
   Unknots. Truth's bellows warm
His hammering at the devil's ribs.

In thirty years with his own
   Fierce flock, his sinning darlings,
   Has he loomed his gold song's
Thread to a holy yet human tone.
Caricature him if you will;
   But do not think your quick lines
   Can catch the grace in his glance
Or scratch the surface of his soul.

He is no dankness in the mind
    of a child nor, huddling, builds
dark memories. His simple kind
    are not finally coffined in fields

of clay but boxed, sunlit, on grass.
    He trembled. His flint-scrubbed
fingers did pruning. His mass
    was neat flower-beds where, robed

in lilac, he fumbled. He picked
    polished apples, then weeded
the plainsong path. Cats licked
    his wrists; fierce dogs tried

to nuzzle. They wanted to put him away
    when he started smiling at bird
and human alike, indiscriminately.
    But he withered and went of his own accord.

DRIVING THROUGH SUTHERLAND

Here too the crofts were burned
To the ground, families stripped
And driven like cattle to the shore.
You can still hear the cursing,
The women shrieking.

                The duke
And his lady sipped port, had
Wax in their ears. Thatch
Blazed. Thistles were torn up
By the root.

          There are men
In Parliament today who could
Be doing more.

              With these thoughts
In mind we drive from Overscaig
To Lairg, through a night as blue
As steel. Leaving Loch Shin behind
We find facing us an even colder
Firth, and a new moon rising
Delicately over a stubble field.

PARK KEEPER

His is a mediaeval landscape, set
In antique colour on a field
Of green, with beds
Of tulips splashed about the shield.

  A silky box-kite rises out
  Of reach of 'where' and 'when';
  A hosepipe turns
  To snake, then doubles back again.

He sits slumped in the sun,
His peaked cap spilling light.
Small boys, like bits
Of paper, weave bright
Circles round him. Till he jerks
To life, becomes quick clown
With one leg dangling. Crazed
As Punch he strikes them down.

  The hosepipe chokes
  The grass it trinkles through;
  The box-kite bumps its cloud
  And disappears into the blue.

Back on his bench, he weeps
His sawdust tears. Dreams sneak
Through tulips, crown him figure
Of fun. Yet he'd not speak
Ungently of them, wish
Them dead; but simply prays: 'Please
Dearest God, don't let them wreck
These perfect tulip beds, or these . . .'

SETTING

Strathglass, a confusion
Of colour. Broom and gorse
Are transfiguration
Of yellow and gold. Furze

Flames, myrtle steeps, is
Its singing fragrance. In
Dusty silences, bees
Are pelted with pollen.

A breathless light
Thins and dribbles,
And haloes a mountain-goat
Maddened by midges. He nimbles

Uphill, but falters as
His shadow crops mine.
Poised, he sees
Me as shambling clown

Invading his own.
Then, gaelic mandarin,
He stilts over the sun.
My gauze shadow is gone.

FERRET

More vicious than stoat or weasel
Because caged, kept hungry, the ferrets
Were let out only for the kill:
An alternative to sulphur and nets.

Once one, badly mauled, hid
Behind a treacle-barrel in the shed.
Throwing me back, Matthew slid
The door shut. From outside

The window, I watched. He stood
Holding an axe, with no gloves.
Then it sprang; and his sleeves
Were drenched in blood

Where the teeth had sunk. I hear
Its high-pitched squeal,
The clamp of its neat steel
Jaws. And I still remember

How the axe flashed, severing
The ferret's head,
And how its body kept battering
The barrels, long after it was dead.

IN A SIMPLE LIGHT

Winter in this place
Is a tangerine sun.
Against the skyline
Nine Shetland ponies

Stand like cut-outs
Fraying at the edges.
Snow puffs and flurries
In weightless driblets

As they platter downhill,
Pink-hooved, chins
Stitched with frost, manes
Jiggling a tinsel trail.

They clutter and jolt,
Are pluff-bellied, biff
Posts, thrum their trough
With warm breathing, smelt

Ice. On the skyline
Again, part fancy, they
Freeze. In each eye
Is a tangerine sun . . .

2

FLIGHT

Leaving the town behind, and the spoiled
  Fields, we made slowly for the hills.
    Our clothes were in rags, our
  Bodies lit with sores. Every
So often we had to water the horse.

Our farm-cart was heaped with straw. Under
    That, the real cargo.
  The soldiers scoffed. After
Searching us, though, they let us through.

We dared not stop, or look round.
  But from the side of the cart
    Came a steady trickle of blood,
Where the most drunken of the guards
  Had run his sword in among the straw.

OUTCAST

These years I have lived
In this hovel, sharing
The smells of others.

Now I have decided
To inhabit my own cave,
Surrounded by my own smell

And that alone. Pungent
As the rest, but more
Familiar. Diogenes

In his barrel lived on scraps
Thrown to the dogs,
The beasts of the field.

He found them amenable,
Having their compensations.
So in his pit the rain-king

Not noticing dead flesh
(It being related to himself)
Finds live meat obnoxious.

I shall return among you
When you have learned
Good sense; when I am able

To control my outrage.
Then my skin will be leather,
My brain warped like a nut.

OMENS AND DISTURBANCES

1   The Gull

A gull lights on Troy. In all its travels
It has seen nothing like this. The beach
Is stained. In the crevices
Of the rocks are nests of fire.
Two armies trumpet on the plain, stopping
Now and again to check on the rules.
The Greeks disembowel a goat, smearing
Their faces with hot entrails.

Or gifts are exchanged: a shield,
A studded belt. Then the spears
Curve, the helmets flash in the sun.
An axe rises and falls; Ajax
Spills men's brains. Every so often
Voices are heard from heaven. The bird
Circles, out of reach of the smoke.
Suddenly it plummets, a white thunderbolt.

2   Helen

The noise and disorder distract me
From my tapestry. It is hot work,
Albeit the point of my needle
Is sharp. See, this done already:
The purple here is Greece; that pale
Green, Troy—held on a single thread.

For weeks now the light has been bad,
A murky orange. I wish they would
Settle things, out there. Still,
With my spices and pomegranates, I am
Moderately contented. Besides, I find
One man's belly very much like another.

3   To Anchises

A few pots, a tinder trail. All that is left
Of Troy. Where are its towers, its boudoirs now?
Hector's skull has been gutted, Priam struck
From behind by those bastards of Greeks.

To reach here I had to wade through gouts
Of blood. Ye gods, Paris will have something
To answer for. That's it, up on to my back.
Truly, this is a fine game we are playing!

4   The Beggar

Let the beggar bend the bow, if he can.
His hair and beard are filthy. Such
A stinkard will not make fools of us.

He can hardly see the axes, never mind
The rings. Old enough to be her father,
And cracked besides. It is Telemachos

Who tries our patience. Not that way,
Dolt, or you break an arm. Once more;
After supper, we shall find other amusement.

RENAISSANCE THOUGHT

Roscelin, at Loches in Brittany,
Held that *man* was not a unity.
This led to trouble about the Trinity:
He recanted, for fear of being burnt for heresy.

Anselm, like a good Platonist, inferred
That a whole which has parts is a mere word.

　To Abelard, nothing secure outside
The Scriptures: even Apostles and Fathers
Could err. An abbot among boors,
　He retired to Cluny where he died.

　　Bernard, an unintelligent saint
　But a man of genuine temperament,
Hated temporal power, became a mystic.
　John of Salisbury, three times secretary
　　To an Archbishop of Canterbury,
Was (in matters outwith the faith) more sceptic.

★

But the real Renaissance is also to be found
In the witches and wizards of mankind:
The iron wheels on which they turned
Did much to liberate the human mind.

THE HALLOWE'EN PARTY

started tamely enough.
Soon the faces
in the tub distorted
to fierce grimaces.
Red apples, bubbling
in a green cauldron.
Cats' entrails
cunningly strewn.
The lanterns guttered.
The boys barred the door.
The girls, free to choose,
became witch or whore.
The room warm as blood . . .

Next morning, they
assumed normality,
said thanks, and drove away.

THE VILLAGERS

They will take over the village.
For them, we shall fashion
Arrowheads, hammers from flint,
Axes from the deer's horn.
They will have us build turf
Walls, a fort every two miles.
Grain will be sown again, milk
Skimmed of its cream. Copper
And tin mixed. We will spread
Dung on the fields. Our women-folk
Will teach them basket-work, how
To stretch boats from hide.

They will study our methods
Of hooking fish, of trampling
Black berries for wine. Before
Each ceremony, they will watch
As we take a cockerel and slit
Its throat over a tin basin.
When we have carved for them
Gods of stone, and set them
On the mountain where our own
Once were, that will be enough.
They will sharpen their knives,
And use our skins for drums.

1

Four knights are stationed at the Fountain
   of Tears, the first day of each month:
   where resides an effigy supporting a unicorn.

They pledge themselves
   to combat of arms: no lady may pass
   unless she give a gage, without a knight
   breaking a lance for her in sport.

A mediaeval game of forfeits.

2

The blessed Philippe, improving
on Francis of Assisi, ordered

that he be laid in a sack,
an iron chain about his neck,

and so placed to die. Then
to be buried naked at the entrance

to the choir, that everyone
might walk over his body, even goats

and dogs. This taking the place
of worldly vanity. *A fine treasure*

for worms.

3
The knight in silver,
   his lady in fur and miniver,
     dance the one dance.

Soon they will be lines
   carved on stone.

    I forget the king's name.

4
Boucicault's piety had a Puritan ring.
He rose early, remained three hours
On his knees at prayer, heard two masses
A day. Dressed in black. Spoke little,

But of God and His Saints. Each
Sunday, made a pilgrimage on foot.
Had read out to him (like Charles)
The lofty histories of Rome.

Was vowed to modesty and chastity.
Virtue the essence of life: a Burgundy
Sparkling with chivalrous ideals.
But the true glory was in the pride.

5

For various impertinences
   the Queen and her ladies
      threatened to beat Scoggin
         with napkins containing stones.

The greatest whore invited
    to strike the first blow . . .

6

It is said that the bodies
   of certain saints
      never decay, being exempt
         from earthly corruption.

That heretics
   have been strictly preserved
      a fortnight, in lime. *Villon*

would have had the nose curve,
   the heart lift the chest . . .

7

The peasants would have slain Romuald
      the Hermit, purely for his bones.

Thomas of Aquinas was decapitated
      by the monks of Fossanuova,
         his relics boiled in a red jar.

[43]

His descendants distributed the ribs
    of Louis, after a great feast.

Elizabeth of Hungary, as she lay
    in state, was stripped and disfigured
    by crowds of worshippers.

At Sienna and Chartres, such splendour.

1 'Flesh swinging from gibbets . . .'

Flesh swinging from gibbets
   by the wayside, in the fastness
      of each shire. In Worcester
the stocks bolted back to back.

Or summarily, in the parks
   and forests of England, yeomen
      whipped and censured
through barons' lickspittle.

Elsewhere, in York, despoiled
   Kent, on sheriffs' tables,
      hands hacked off at the wrist.
Venison a king's dish.

2 Excavation

To each layer, its knight
   or yeoman; each area
      its detail of death: axe
haft or sword hilt laid there.

So, the trench dug,
   centuries compressed
      in Sussex dust. Deepest
a Norman, the skull lost.

Then a monk (the abbey site
    close by) buried
        complete with crucifix
and chain. That in proud

Henry's time. So we study
    this passage of chivalry;
        forgetting we ourselves
are measured here already.

3 *St. George's Day*

To each his duty: whether the plate
    to polish, casque to comb and feather,
        metal to temper and trim. Outside,
war on shaded Savoie, France's fields.

Throughout Europe, to each his station:
    manor for lord and lady, barn and straw
        for beast and serf. The leavings
from the table passed round, cold swill.

In the midst of this, he tried taking
    the shire by the ears, whipping those
        who were slow, scoring pale flesh, making
mock of the simple, for ladies' laughter.

Till at last, on St. George's day, the parks
    prepared for the tourney, they fastened
        him in his armour, tied and placed him
on his caparisoned beast. Not till too late,

[46]

at the oven gates, did he realise
   how they hated him—as, locked
      behind his visor, they raised
the grill and thrust him in to roast . . .

STYLE

So often I have heard you say you wished
You had been born in Roman times—or Greek.
You dream of columns, cool façades,
Of fountains playing in a classic shade.

Much to suit your eye for purity, your poise.
But there might have been another side
To it all: not Christians being mauled, arenas
Crawling with maggots—nothing so crude.

Just that, if you'd been born into that age,
Some ironic fate would have made
You still the object of my love and hate:
Myself Catullus, mawkish at your side.

TWO SONNETS

The Knight

We sensed someone was coming: in the yard
The horses were straining and snorting
As in Dostoevsky. No way of stopping
Him: we had left no-one on guard.

He stood there, at first obscurely
Then growing more and more clear. His helmet
Glowed as only gold can, purely.
He wore a cloak of richest velvet,

And his beard was frizzled. At least
I thought he had a beard, but
Afterwards the others said no. He must
Have told us many things that night;

Yet I remember only, in his eye,
Rembrandt's unutterable lapis lazuli.

Rilke

To the age of five his mother kept
Him in girlish clothes, his hair
Plaited. At ten he was given
The emperor's uniform to wear.

Later in life he grew less partial
To the gay tunic, its tight
Buttons. In a helmet of gold
He drove wild horses through the night.

It took an angel finally to mould him.
His head sucked dry of its storm,
He began posing before mirrors—
Absolving himself from his own form.

At the end he simply plucked a rose:
This brought the saga-cycle to a close.

MARGINS

It is one thing to talk of terror
In the abstract, quite another
To face up to the particular,
Fencing in the feeling of fear.

To speak, say, of a mother
Whose breast is touched by tumour;
Or the less explicit horror
Of a brother's mental disorder.

And most of all, in a rare
Moment, to explain to a daughter
What margins are: the nature
Of the charmed lives we bear.

THE FORTS

The sites of the forts
Are still there, rings
Of vitrified stone, stratum
On stratum, where wood blazed.

Whether for strength,
The walls for endurance,
Or by the enemy from outside
(To roast men) no-one knows.

As, the imprint of skull
On stone, mark of shoulder
And thigh in an earthen gallery,
In sleep or by the invader's sword.

And I am as good as there
Already, with these, in that
place. My bones neatly
Longwise, the skull cleft and plated.

Whether by age or rock-fall,
In peace or by brutal assault,
Spite or knowledge of man, will
Matter then not in the least.

THREE CIRCUS POEMS

Lion-Tamer
So, the hot breath, the ring round me
Of haunch and mane, the eye always on me.
Strop of muscular shoulder, the easy
Stride, tail switching the sawdust up.
The jaws foremost in my mind—which take
Flesh, drip flame: could at no notice
A man's sinews snap, like a clown
Draw me tattered through a paper hoop.

Not skill, but knowledge. Of the fiery
Bowl, the fierce flower that's lion.
Attention caught. The soft paw. Giant
Cat. Who's met, who's held, who's master.
The one danger (and lion can sense it)
That the mind slip from its ring
To where the crowd sits, tier upon tier,
Its breath fetid, hungering for the killing.

Clown
Week in, week out, over half England. Folk
Laughing their ruddy heads off. My world
A paper hoop, coloured balls, a plastic
Smile. Beginning to get past it, though.
Mean to say, it knocks me out. You try
Being up a ladder one minute, the next flat
On your face. Fancy a turn on the stilts?
Or having cold water squirted up your pants?

Okay for the seven-and-sixes. But how
About me? My eyes itching, gut stuck
With straw, sweat in my armpits pricking.
What you could call scratching a living.
Had a couple of goes at the telly: interviewed,
And that. Ruined my chances, ask me.
'This bloke you're always on about' I said,
'This bloke Hamlet—who the ruddy hell's he?'

Elephant-Girl

Like I keep trying to tell you, just
An ordinary girl. This maharanee
Stuff, that's strictly for the show . . .
Yes, Shettleston, my mum tells me.
The usual tastes, what do you mean?
The leather gear's for the act, see.
That's right, the boots too. Look
Ducky, there's nothing kinky about me.

The circus? No choice. Born into it,
Like I said. In the blood. Talk
And breathe elephants. Sat
On their backs before I could walk . . .
That's right, develops the muscles.
Could be dangerous, I suppose. Never think
About it. Elephants is like people, you see:
Okay, so long as you can take the stink.

ESSENTIALS

The sad thing is that the trees will go.

When the expressway is built, the double
Line down each side will be torn up
And destroyed, not replanted. This is how
They work, stripping land to a minimum.

What a pity planners cannot pare to essentials
Like Giacometti, leaving behind what counts.

THE FOX IN HIS LAIR...

The fox in his lair
by oak-root and whorl
is presence, not scent
of fox. Is cold fury
of fur—soft pad
of cunning by night.

The badger in his burrow
no fairy-tale brock,
but paw crooked like a nut
ready to tear
the earth's skin
to get at the bone.

The raven, sweeping
in air, no line
on a blue plate: but
gorger of carrion, meat
in his gullet, slivers
trailing from each talon.

And you, my sweet,
how can you hope
to convince me
you are all sweetness—
when I know where
your hands have burrowed?

Like badger, like raven
and fox, who inhabit
domains of their own
in air, you are
no mere colour or scent;
but of the earth, your rotten lair.

RIMBAUD, HARAR

So, mother, you have not changed after
All. I had thought something, here

And there, after all those years . . .
Well, as you see, I am now near

To death. Isabel, burn these letters:
They are from some imbecile in Paris.

Yes, my leg has been amputated—as
I cut off that part of myself

That gave birth to poems. I see life
In different colours. I am almost ready

To be received into the Church. (That
Will please you, mother.) Though I don't

Know how I shall get down on my hands
And knees, there have been such forces

At work. Not true, what they will tell
You, about the women here. Do you know,

The violins have never stopped playing—
Not once in all those years . . .

Soon I shall be heading for Paris.
For the last time. One journey I shall

Not have to bother about, no matter
What drunken fools are carrying the litter.

AMBUSH

Most of the night we rode, guns at our backs
And our hands tied, so that when the beasts stumbled
We had to grip by the knees or be thrown. Our wrists
    Turned to wire. The blood froze.
Twice we were signalled to stop. Then
    They gave us scraps, a mouthful of water each.

We had almost reached the clearing when it came.
My horse, one of the first to be hit, went down.
Another landed on top, its flanks bubbling.
    Branches were sawn by fire. My mouth
Filled with blood. We had been ambushed
    By our own side. Unable to move, I blacked out.

The next day, it was spring. Trees were traced
Against an elegant sky. Without getting up
I tried to remember the dream. I found
    My hands still tied. And there,
Stripped and dripping like stoats in the sunlight,
    Were eight men fastened through the throat to trees.